JOYOUS *Journey* OF LOSS

Finding Joy in the Midst of Difficult Circumstances

JOYOUS Journey OF LOSS

Finding Joy in the Midst of Difficult Circumstances

TAMATHA A. DAVIS

CONTRIBUTING AUTHORS

Alecia Baptiste, Carmella Culp, April Foster,
Marian Hogan, and Melisa Miles

ISBN 978-1-7330579-0-5

Sivad Publishing
PO Box 62328
Houston, TX 77205

Printed in USA by Ingram Spark

First printing, August, 2019

Unless otherwise indicated, Scripture quotations are taken from the New American Standard Bible® (NASB), Copyright © 1960, 1962, 1963, 1968, 1971, 1972, 1973, 1975, 1977, 1995 by The Lockman Foundation. Used by permission. www.Lockman.org

Cover & Interior Design by Jonathan Lewis, Jonlin Creative

Author Photos: Mercy and Grace Photography

Floral Arrangement on Table: iStock.com/MonicaNinker

Coffee Cup: Jan Alexander from Pixabay

ACKNOWLEDGEMENTS

This book would not be possible without my Lord and Savior Jesus Christ. I am so thankful that He chose me. When I was lost and deep in sin, He rescued me from the path of destruction that I was on. Thank you Lord for your grace and your mercy. It is in you that I live and move and have my being!

No one has been a bigger cheerleader for every endeavor I undertake than my husband Michael. Thank you for being there for me, providing wisdom, insight into scripture, and comic relief. After 24 years of marriage and all its ups and downs, sometimes you just have to laugh!

Thanks to my four amazing children—QJ, Michael, Miles, and Zoe and my one spectacular granddaughter—Miracle! You five humans are my heartbeat, and I do not know what I would do without you.

My mother, Marian Hogan, never left my side during my two-month hospital stay and time in rehab. She has been a constant friend, confidant and supporter throughout my whole life, but especially during this season of losing my leg.

And last, but certainly not least, I want to thank my beautiful lioness prayer team who through their prayers and support gave me the inspiration to write this book: Alecia Baptiste, Catherine Brasel, Carmella Culp, April Foster, Helen Lee, Melisa Miles, Randie Ward and Anita Wilson. Some of their stories are in this book, and some are not. There are many others who have supported me through prayer, finances, visits, bringing food, and a myriad of other ways. I thank each and every one of you. You know who you are.

Thank you to my editor, John Carpenter, who has an eagle's eye. You are fabulous at what you do!

PREFACE

This book began over a decade ago as an idea about the trials that all women endure silently. There is a secret code among women that we do not share our real problems with each other. We do not discuss what is really going on. In fact, we attempt to wear a mask to cover up what is really happening and has happened in our lives. Thankfully, a few brave women break the code. I, along with some friends, have decided to join that elite class of brave women who have decided to unmask themselves. Maybe after reading this book you will decide to join us.

I began putting pen to paper during my two-month stay in the hospital after the loss of my leg. It was amputated above the knee due to a rare vascular disorder which led to poor circulation in my extremities. As I lay there, I began to realize that even though I had suffered this tremendous loss, I still had joy.

Then I began to reflect on the other losses I experienced throughout my more than 40 years of life. No matter what I said or how I behaved, everyone knew that I had lost my leg. They also knew that I had lost my home and many of my possessions when Hurricane Harvey hit Houston in 2017. Prior to that I lost my hearing.

In that moment I saw the pattern that had been created in my life. I was on a journey of loss! Whenever I thought I was free and clear..."bam!" something else would happen, and I would lose something else. Then I realized that I was not on this journey alone. There were other women who had endured losses. My job was to bring them together, break the secret code of masking our problems, and share our testimonies of loss in this book to help thousands of other women break free and have joy in the midst of their losses.

As I was going through the most difficult loss I had ever faced—the loss of my leg—the Lord sent an amazing group of powerful prayer warriors to pray me through. I knew that these were the women who would unmask themselves and share their greatest loss just like me.

In the process of enduring that loss, God has given me joy. This book will not only unmask the difficulties and trials that real women face in secret, it will also give you the tools to walk through those losses with joy. Join me on this journey, and the next time you find yourself facing a loss you will be able to endure it and come out on the other side with joy!

The purpose of this book and my heartfelt desire is to encourage women that no matter what you have lost through your trials, you can still have joy. No matter the pain that you may have had to endure, you can still have joy. In the midst of your journey of loss you can still have joy!

TABLE OF CONTENTS

INTRODUCTION

Have you ever lost something? I mean something that you really value. You are ambling along with all of your possessions in place and then all of a sudden you realize something is missing. Along the way, you lost something. Many times this can be a gut-wrenching blow to your psyche as you try to retrace your steps to figure out at which point you lost it. You go over and over in your mind how things would be different had you not lost it. Where was the misstep? How could I have done things differently to avoid losing it? You come back repeatedly to the same devastating conclusion, however.

It is lost.

It is gone.

Sometimes the loss is completely out of your control, and there is nothing you could have done differently. Apart from the feeling of helplessness, this type of loss somehow feels better because you do not get to blame yourself for the loss. When someone dies, you know you had nothing to do with that loss so somehow it is more palatable.

Sadly, in our journey called life, we will face many losses whether we had some semblance of control in it or not. We will realize time and time again as we are walking through our life, *"Wait, something is missing!"*

We will search and search, but we will not be able to find it. Or the thing that we lose will be stripped from us—ripped out of our hands leaving us in utter despair and sadness as we cry out, *"Why? Why did I have to lose this?*

"God, why did you take this from me?"

We know that He is sovereign in all things, so it often feels like He is taking something from us. The reality is that we live in a fallen world. When Adam and Eve sinned, we all became recipients of loss. The idea of loss was brought into humanity when they ate of the tree that God told them not to eat from. And now we live with those consequences from The Fall everyday.

Since loss is unavoidable in this life, it's best for us to at least learn to deal with it. That's what this book is about. It is about finding a sustaining joy in Jesus in the midst of our losses.

It is also about opening ourselves up to share with others about those losses in the hope that we can help someone along the way. Jesus even said, "In the world you have tribulation, but take courage; I have overcome the world." (John 16:33b). Tribulation also means trouble, difficulty, problem, worry, anxiety, burden, cross to bear, ordeal, trial, adversity, hardship, tragedy, sorrow, loss, trauma, affliction. Jesus never promised that our life would be free from those things, only that we could overcome them with Him. In this book, we share some of our losses and give you the tools on how to overcome yours with joy!

HOW TO READ THIS BOOK

Read Part 1: *My Journey* and Part 3: *Brave Women Unmask Themselves* in order to build up your courage to unmask yourself and recognize that you are not alone.

Study Part 2: *Steps to Having A Joyous Journey.* This section gives you the details and specifics on having a joyous journey in the midst of loss.

Get involved in Part 4: *It's Your Turn* by sharing your loss.

Do the work in Part 5 : *The Toolbox.*

1. Carefully read through each tool.
2. Go back and read it out loud. These are scripture passages, prayers and confessions.
3. Write as much of the tools as you can on small note cards that you can keep with you in your Bible, your purse or your prayer room.
4. Read as much as you can aloud daily.
5. Make it your goal to memorize the scriptures, prayers and confessions

PART I:
MY JOURNEY

Loss of a Parent
The Father I Never Knew

Loss of Love
Too Young to Die

Loss of My Leg
My New Normal

LOSS OF A PARENT

The Father I Never Knew

My parents were not married, so I was born into loss—the loss of my father. As a little girl, and even through my teenage years and early adulthood, I did not understand nor realize the significant void in my life caused by not having a father. I must stop here and honor my mother, Marian Hogan. She raised me along with her twin sister, Marilyn Rice.

Throughout my childhood, I can say that I never lacked for anything. I now understand that the Lord was protecting me from the pain of rejection and abandonment until I was old enough and mature enough in Him to deal with those emotions. I still must acknowledge my mom because although my father never gave her a dime in child support nor did he ever give me a gift for birthdays or Christmas; she never spoke one negative word about him. I know this sounds crazy, but because of that, it was easier for me to walk through life never seeing the gaping hole—the loss of a parent.

With that being said, there are things that I did because of the loss that I didn't understand at the time. Looking back, it all makes sense. I was extremely promiscuous , and I realize now that I simply wanted the love of a man. Sadly, I was willing to do whatever it took to get it.

Fathers set the standards for their daughters on what type of man will be allowed into their life. Because no one was there to set that standard, many of my relationships included emotional and physical abuse. These disastrous consequences were the result of a loss that I didn't even know I was experiencing. It was due to the loss of my father—the father I never knew.

I am so thankful that God sent my husband when I was only 18. He actually rescued me from my last abuser. I would no longer have to endure more physical and emotional abuse as an adult.

When I was in my mid-20s, the whole facade came crashing down. I remember the day like it was yesterday. I saw my father in person less than five times and talked to him on the phone even less than that. However, for some reason he decided to call me on his birthday. We chatted for a while. I remember feeling a little bothered by the fact that he had never called me on my birthday, and yet here he was calling on his. Did he expect something from me? A gift? Money? Why was he calling me? I hung up the phone and a sadness like I had never experienced enveloped me.

When I was in my mid-20s, the whole facade came crashing down.

The next day I went to my ladies' Bible study still sad, but I really did not know why. I asked for prayer. My prayer request went something like this, *"Could you all pray for me? Ever since I talked to my father yesterday, I have been feeling sad. We are not close. I don't have a relationship with him."*

Well these precious women began to pray for me. They were praying things like, *"Lord, please reconcile Tamatha with her father. Draw them closer together."* During the prayer I wanted to yell out and tell them, *"No!"* I wanted them to stop praying because I did not ask for any of that. I just wanted the sadness to go away.

In that moment I realized that I had issues with my father. I was responding this way because I finally recognized the loss in my life. I saw the gaping hole, and I saw my brokenness. I saw myself as a sad, abandoned, rejected, little girl all alone with no one to protect her. I felt the pain of rejection that the Lord had so graciously protected me from. I was ready to face it. I was ready to acknowledge my loss—the loss of my father.

After that the Lord took me on a journey of healing. He healed the pain of rejection from my father. He healed the pain of aban-donment. Eventually, I was able to pursue a real, lasting relationship with my father. I remember going to his home, cooking him a meal and really honoring the position he held in my life as my father. Although he never did anything a father would do, the Lord led me to honor his position.

Sadly, our relationship was short-lived because he passed away from a brain aneurysm about two years later. I am thankful that the Lord restored our relationship in time for me to honor him and get to know him a little before he died. I have joy when I reflect on the time I spent with him at the end of his life.

LOSS OF LOVE

Too Young to Die

Be strong and courageous, do not be afraid or tremble
at them, for the Lord your God is the one who goes with
you. He will not fail you or forsake you.
(DEUTERONOMY 31:6)

When I was 12 years old, I fell in love. He was the boy that lived next door to my grandmother. I lived in Houston with my mother, and he lived in Austin with his mother. However, every summer he went to stay with his father, and I went to stay with my grandmother in a sleepy little town in southeast Texas.

We did everything together. We fished, ate at the Dairy Queen, played at the park, sometimes snuck out at night to talk and take long walks through the streets of our little town. We just had fun like normal 12-year-old kids. Our relationship was pure. It was innocent. It was beautiful.

By the time I was 16, I knew that I wanted to marry him. He was the love of my life. He was kind, generous and funny. There was just the infectious joy about him that made everyone want to be around him. His laugh was loud, beautiful, unfiltered and contagious; it made me weak in the knees. I would do anything for him.

In early September of our sixteenth year, my aunt and uncle had a big party. Everyone in that little town went to that party, even the kids. I remember walking around the party looking for him. Once I found him, we got into an argument and I walked away. He called after me, but I never turned around. That would be the last time I saw him alive. A while later I heard gunshots. What I learned is that two guys were fighting, and one pulled out a gun. My boyfriend jumped between them and was fatally shot in the stomach.

Yes, fatally.

He died.

He was 16.

Devastated is not even the word to describe how I felt. I did not speak for two whole days. After that my mother considered taking me to a therapist because I was so sad.

This great loss changed me forever.

Every night I dreamed of him. He would call me on the phone and ask me to meet him somewhere—one of the places that we used to frequent. In the dream I could never make it to him. Most nights I woke up crying as I realized once again that he would never call me on the phone again. We would never go for walks, and he would never be my husband or boyfriend for that matter.

I cried because I knew the only time I would visit him again would be at the cemetery where we left him in that shiny blue box, eyes closed, fake placid grin on his face.

"Why was he smiling?" I wanted to ask the funeral people but I remained silent in my grief after passing out when I saw him lying there so still and quiet, like he was sleeping.

But we all knew he was never waking up.

Dead.

At 16.

This great loss changed me forever.

I was.

Never.

The same.

In all honesty, I do not know how I made it through this loss. This was the first big one. I had recently given my life to the Lord, so I was just a baby Christian. I knew nothing of what it meant to have joy amid trials and suffering. All I knew was that I missed him terribly, and I wanted him back. Even in my infancy, God did meet me right where I was with His peace. He sustained me. He held me. He walked with me. He never left me for one moment, and for that I am thankful. I eventually found joy and love again. I have been happily married for almost 25 years.

LOSS OF MY LEG

My New Normal

So that the proof of your faith, being more precious than
gold which is perishable, even though tested by fire, may
be found to result in praise and glory and honor at the
revelation of Jesus Christ;

(1 PETER 1:7)

In August of 2017, we lost our home in Harvey. This began an almost two-year journey to find stability amid chaos. My family and I, which at that time included my husband, two teenage sons, my daughter and one-year old granddaughter lived in a hotel for six months. Actually, it was a really nice hotel, but it was not home.

During that time, I noticed that at certain times it was difficult for me to walk. I began having excruciating pain in my legs and began spending most of my days in bed. I had to travel sometimes for work and I found myself requesting wheelchair assistance at the airport because I just could not make it to my gate. Little did I know that the arteries in my legs were slowly closing and cutting off the blood supply to my extremities.

In May we moved out of the hotel and three members of my family myself included graduated. I pursued a degree in Communications. My husband graduated from seminary and my son from high school, by way of homeschooling I might add. I planned a huge graduation party for the three of us. So much was going on that by the time I got back around to all the testing my doctors had asked me to complete it was too late.

They could not save it.

I lost...my leg.

My right leg was amputated above the knee. I spent almost two months in the hospital and two weeks in a rehab facility. It was while I was in the hospital that the Lord began to speak to me about this book. I told my husband that I was going to write a book about losing my leg.

They could not save it.

I said, *"It will be called Journey of Loss."*
Immediately my husband said, *"No! Joyous Journey of Loss".*
And he was right!

I finally came home to my new normal in a wheelchair. I cannot describe the intensity of this loss. However, to my amazement I still had joy! I recognized early on that I could control my atmosphere. By filling it with praise and taking negative thoughts captive immediately, I lived in a place where I experienced the peace and joy of God.

So many people told me I was an inspiration, but I never felt like that. I was only walking through my trial in the way that God called me to walk through it - with joy!

My whole life changed. I had to relearn how to do everything. In many ways I felt helpless while in other areas I felt empowered. God has been by my side every moment. He never allowed me to wallow in self-pity but provided a continuous stream of joy by the Holy Spirit!

As an amputee, I am fully active again doing all the things I once did, just now with a prosthetic leg. It is different, and I've had to learn many things over again, but I would not trade my place in Christ for anything.

During this time my children, my husband, and I have grown in ways unimaginable, and I believe this would not have happened without the loss of my leg. According to scripture, trials come to make us stronger and to mature us in the faith. "Consider it all joy, my brethren, when you encounter various trials, knowing that the testing of your faith produces endurance. And let endurance have *its* perfect result, so that you may be perfect and complete, lacking in nothing. (James 1:2-4)

It sounds strange, but I do thank and praise God for all He has allowed in my life. He is sovereign, and His plans for me are for my good and His glory. I have real and sustaining joy!

PART II: STEPS TO HAVING A JOY JOURNEY

You are not Alone

Unmask Yourself

Stay Praised Up

Your Mind is Your Battlefield

Awaken to the Joy Within You

You Are Not Alone

Do not fear, for I am with you; Do not anxiously look about
you, for I am your God. I will strengthen you, surely I will
help you, Surely I will uphold you with My righteous right
hand.

(Isaiah 41:10)

We want people to think that the beautiful home we live in on the right side of the tracks in the very best neighborhood has never been in foreclosure. We would never let anyone know that we are struggling to pay the mortgage every month because we probably couldn't afford it in the first place. Our tall, athletically-built husband with the model's good looks doesn't have a wandering eye. Nor has he been unemployed more than he's been employed during our marriage.

And don't forget our beautiful, amazing, perfect, smart children. We don't want people to know that our son dropped out of college. Or that our daughter's recent trip down south was not just to visit family. It was because she was pregnant, and one of our relatives is helping find a home for the baby. We are always smiling and in a seemingly good mood, but no one knows we have to take antidepressants just to get through each day.

These are not the topics of polite conversation. So instead we just keep it all to ourselves. Slowly we affix the mask over our face with its phony smile and vacant eyes. It's too embarrassing.

They don't have problems like mine.

No one does.

No one will understand.

I am alone....

The truth is you are not alone. Not only do you have a loving Heavenly Father who will never leave you or forsake you, there are many women that have walked the same or a similar path as you have. There is nothing new under the sun. Another woman has endured the suffering you are experiencing right now and survived. She's come out on the other side with scars, but she is stronger and better.

Remember the thing that you thought might kill you didn't. It made you stronger. Look at yourself. You do not look like what you've been though!

Remember the three Hebrew boys in Daniel 3. Shadrach, Meshach and Abednego. They were thrown into the fiery furnace because they would not bow to the statue of King Nebuchadnezzar.

Do life's situations and circumstances make you feel like you are in the fire? Well, in this instance the king ordered the fire turned up 10 times hotter and even the king's assistants, who were there, were burned to death. However, the Bible records that when the three Hebrew boys came out of the fire, their clothes did not smell of smoke and not a hair on their head was singed. That's you! He will deliver you in such a way that you will not even look like what you've been through.

That's why many of us don't share those victories. Since we do not look like what we have been through, why bring it up? No one wears their testimony on their sleeve. I'll just keep this mask on. I'll keep covering up my problems. I'll keep walking in darkness. I'll keep my brokenness to myself. I won't ask for help. No, it's okay. I'm good. In truth you are keeping yourself and other women from getting their victory because they believe the lie that they are alone just like you do.

No matter what it is, you are not alone. Do not hide behind shame and embarrassment. Recognize that you are not the only one going through this trial. Do not allow yourself to be isolated in your pain, because when you are isolated negative thoughts begin to creep into your mind.

Recognize that you are not alone. The enemy loves it when we think we are alone. That is when he attacks with vengeance. You begin to think you have no one to talk to and that no one will understand. Someone WILL understand. You are not alone.

UNMASK YOURSELF

And they overcame him because of the blood of the Lamb
and because of the word of their testimony, and they did not
love their life even when faced with death.
(REVELATION 12:11)

The time has finally come for truth telling. You must begin to unmask yourself. Being completely honest about your journey is the only way to find joy in the midst of it. There is a level of wisdom and discernment required when telling your story. You are not just going to shout it from the rooftops to anyone who will listen. As you trust God, He will reveal who to release your truth to. He will show the friend that is ready to meet the real you—the unmasked you. The you that you've kept hidden for a very long time.

Women are most concerned with what other women think of them. Oftentimes the beginning of unmasking yourself is realizing that what others think of me is none of my business! That's a hard concept to grasp.

Humility is not thinking less of yourself, it's simply thinking of yourself less. If we want to begin to walk in truth about who we really are, this is one of the first steps. The Bible says in James

4:10 "Humble yourselves in the presence of the Lord, and He will exalt you."

Don't worry about what others think about your house, your car, your children, your husband or any of your possessions. If they judge you for those things, it is doubtful that they were real friends to begin with. Don't even think about those things. Instead, "Set your mind on the things above, not on the things that are on earth." (Colossians 3:2)

As we focus on spiritual things, impressing other people becomes less and less important. In this way, we do not love our lives unto death as the Scripture states. This will free us up to begin unmasking ourselves. Who cares if you are in debt and your family is not perfect? Chances are they are in debt too, and no one's family is perfect. So let go of the facade you have been keeping up. Let go of the lies and half-truths you've been telling to make yourself look good for others. In short, take off the mask!

When you do begin to unmask yourself, you will experience a joy that you've never known. In that process you will help other women to experience it as they begin to unmask themselves. The joy will be insatiable and contagious. It will spread like wildfire. Unable to be contained, it will break down walls of shame and embarrassment erected decades ago and allow the sweet ministry of the Holy Spirit to come in.

Stay Praised Up

O clap your hands, all peoples; Shout to God with the voice
of joy.
(Psalm 47:1)

People have told you to stay prayed up. Well, I submit to you that you also need to stay praised up. Throughout your day, play worship music, sing and worship the King. This helps you to keep your focus on Him and not on your circumstances. As you begin to lift Him up higher and higher in your praise, the seemingly insurmountable problems and circumstances you are facing become smaller and smaller. Hebrews 12:1 tells us. "fixing our eyes on Jesus, the author and perfecter of faith, who for the joy set before Him endured the cross, despising the shame, and has sat down at the right hand of the throne of God."

As we gaze at Jesus in all of His splendor and beauty, we begin to look at Him and meditate on what He did for us in going to the cross. That truth will begin to saturate every part of our being. Although our circumstances may not immediately change, sweet sister, we will change! We will be filled with a peace and a joy that is immeasurable! We will be caught up in the presence of God. Our focus will shift from the things of this world to the things of heaven.

The Bible records the story of Paul and Silas when they were imprisoned. I have never been in prison, but I can imagine that it must be a pretty low point in a person's life. And yet the Bible records that while in prison Paul and Silas were singing and praising God, and in the midst of that God sent an earthquake to release them from prison.

But about midnight Paul and Silas were praying and singing hymns of praise to God, and the prisoners were listening to them; and suddenly there came a great earthquake, so that the foundations of the prison house were shaken; and immediately all the doors were opened and everyone's chains were unfastened. (Acts 16:25-26)

God will release you from your prison as you begin to praise him—your prison of depression and sadness—your prison fear. The bondage is broken as you begin to praise and worship God, just like Paul and Silas.

Your Mind is Your Battlefield

For the weapons of our warfare are not of the flesh, but
divinely powerful for the destruction of fortresses. We are
destroying speculations and every lofty thing raised up
against the knowledge of God, and we are taking every
thought captive to the obedience of Christ.

(2 Corinthians 10:4)

Your mind is your battlefield. Negative thoughts can wreak havoc on our mind. According to research[1], negative thoughts make up 80% of the 12,000 to 60,000 thoughts we have each day, 95% of which we had the day before. Basically, we are having the same 9,600 to 48,000 negative thoughts everyday. This is what has to stop! We have to take control of our minds and recognize that this is where the battle for our joy is taking place.

The analogy of a warrior, battle or soldier is used many times in Scripture. All things considered, maybe God wants us to realize that we are in a battle.

---

[1]https://faithhopeandpsychology.wordpress.com/2012/03/02/80-of-thoughts-are-negative-95-are-repetitive/

Once we realize that we are in a battle and we have a very real enemy, then we can begin to fight. However, we do not fight in the natural world, but in the Spirit. Our only offensive weapon is the Word of God. This is where knowing our Bible comes in handy. When the negative thoughts come into our minds, we have to cast them down with the Word of God. The bible says *"We are destroying speculations and every lofty thing raised up against the knowledge of God, and **we are** taking every thought captive to the obedience of Christ,"* (2 Corinthians 10:5). Do not allow negative thoughts to just linger in your mind. Find a verse which represents the truth in that situation and pray and confess that scripture passage until the thought goes away.

For example, if your thought is something like *"I am all alone. No one cares about me."* As soon as that thought pops into your head say, *"God says He will never leave me or forsake me."* (Hebrews 13:5) and *"God cares for me because His many thoughts towards me are precious."* (Psalm 139:16-17)

Sometimes you have to say it out loud so that you can hear yourself saying God's Word because faith comes by hearing. (Romans 10:17) As you begin confessing God's Word over your life, you will notice that your thought life will begin to change. Scripture says, "For as he thinks within himself, so he is...." (Proverbs 23:7a).

The spiritual world is just as real as the natural world—only we cannot see it. Remember the story of Elisha, his servant, and the Arameans? The King of Aram was at war with Israel. He was enraged when he found out that Elisha was the prophet informing the King of Israel on how to battle him effectively, so he sent an army to Dothan. The army surrounded the city that night to capture Elisha. When Elisha and his servant awoke the next morning, they knew they were surrounded. Elisha's servant questioned him.

"Then Elisha prayed and said, 'O LORD, I pray, open his eyes that he may see.' And the LORD opened the servant's eyes and he saw; and behold, the mountain was full of horses and chariots of fire all around Elisha." (2 Kings 6:17) God sent an army of angels to do battle on Elisha's behalf!

We read these verses in Daniel 10:12b-13 "...Daniel, for from the first day that you set your heart on understanding *this* and on humbling yourself before your God, your words were heard, and I have come in response to your words. But the prince of the kingdom of Persia was withstanding me for twenty-one days; then behold, Michael, one of the chief princes, came to help me, for I had been left there with the kings of Persia."

We are reading an account of a battle between an angel and a demonic force—the king of Persia—taking place in the spiritual realm. The spiritual battle that was happening was so fierce that the angel could not reach Daniel with the answer to his prayer until another angel named Michael came to his aid.

There is a real spiritual battle being fought! Use the weapon that you have been given which is the Word of God. In Psalm 103:20 Scripture tells us, "Bless the LORD, you His angels, Mighty in strength, who perform His word, Obeying the voice of His word." The angels respond to the Word of God! As you speak His Word, by using your offensive weapon, God will fight your battles as well as He did for Elijah and Daniel.

Awaken To the Joy Within You

But in all these things we overwhelmingly conquer through
Him who loved us. For I am convinced that neither death,
nor life, nor angels, nor principalities, nor things present,
nor things to come, nor powers, nor height, nor depth, nor
any other created thing, will be able to separate us from the
love of God, which is in Christ Jesus our Lord.

(Romans 8:37-39)

Awaken to the joy within you! When you become a Christian, God puts His spirit on the inside of you—the Holy Spirit. The Holy Spirit has fruit. Another word for fruit could be attributes. There are certain attributes or ways of behavior you will exhibit because God's Spirit is living inside you. "But the fruit of the Spirit is love, joy, peace, patience, kindness, goodness, faithfulness, gentleness, self-control; against such things there is no law." (Galatians 5:22-23) Joy is one of the fruits of the Spirit. However, if your spirit man is weak, you may not be experiencing that fruit. That is where strengthening your inner man through worship, prayer and reading God's Word is necessary.

If you want to awaken to the joy within you:

- **Recognize that You Are Not Alone:** There is nothing new under the sun. Do not allow the enemy to isolate you by tricking you into believing that no one has ever gone through what you are going through.
- **Unmask Yourself:** Stop hiding who you really are with lies and half-truths. Share your REAL testimony. Take off the mask!
- **Stay Praised Up:** Worship God in song. Keep your focus on Him instead of your circumstances.
- **Recognize that your mind is the battlefield:** Stop allowing negative thoughts to permeate your mind. Begin to speak or confess God's Word out of your mouth to bring down the lies of the enemy.

All of these steps already discussed will lead you to your joyous journey as the joy on the inside of you becomes alive.

One important thing to note is that this is not about laughter. Laughter can be an indicator that you have joy just like speaking in tongues can be an indicator that your have the Holy Spirit. Consider this. Many people that have the Holy Spirit do not speak in tongues, and in the same way many can have joy and are not doubled over in laughter at every moment of the day.

Joy goes beyond laughter. Laughter is momentary and temporary, but joy is sustaining and enduring. Laughter is often circumstantial, but circumstances are irrelevant when you have joy. You can have joy while you get ready for work, clean your home, cook dinner or put your children to bed. It is on the inside and governs your actions and how you navigate this world. It is the sustaining power of the Holy Spirit given to strengthen you for life's trials.

God may allow the trial in your life, but He will also give you everything you need to endure it. "No temptation has overtaken you but such as is common to man; and God is faithful, who will not allow you to be tempted beyond what you are able, but with the temptation will provide the way of escape also, so that you will be able to endure it." (1 Corinthians 10:13)

"Seeing that His divine power has granted to us everything pertaining to life and godliness, through the true knowledge of Him who called us by His own glory and excellence." (1 Peter 1:3)

May God be your strength as you embark on your joy journey. "And He has said to me, "My grace is sufficient for you, for power is perfected in weakness." (2 Corinthians 12:9)

PART III:
BRAVE WOMEN UNMASK THEMSELVES

Loss of Innocence
Unprotected

Loss of Freedom
Bound to Be Free

Loss of A Dream
Family or Fiancée'

Loss of Significance
Rainbow in the Sky

Loss of Identity
Losing Big Two

Loss of A Son
The Fight for My Life

Loss of Trust
Broken Vows

LOSS OF INNOCENCE

Unprotected

Trust in the Lord with all your heart, and lean not on your
own understanding; in all your ways acknowledge Him, and
He shall direct your paths.
(PROVERBS 3:5-6, NKJV)

It was a bright sunny Saturday afternoon. I was all dressed up in my Sunday best with pigtails, tights and patent-leather shoes. I had just enough time to go play at my friend's house before the photo shoot. After getting permission, I left. Even though she wasn't home, I remained in the courtyard of her apartment building for what seemed like an eternity. I was just far enough from my own apartment complex that no one could see me. When I heard my father's whistle, I knew I'd better come running or I'd be in big trouble. I knew that meant the man had arrived. I thought, *if I stay here long enough, maybe the man in the big white car will leave.* I was right! Shortly after he left, I returned home. *"Didn't you hear me whistling for you?"* My dad said.

I simply acted as if I had been inside and was unaware of his multiple, high-pitched tones demanding that I return home immediately. *Didn't they know I didn't want to go?* I couldn't understand why they were sending me with him again! Unfortunately, he returned a little later, and no matter how much I cried, they forced me to leave with him, the man that my parents called "boss".

Sadly, my parents had been duped into thinking their boss was taking me to his apartment all alone to take photographs of me in a pretty dress for the paper. He was supposedly taking pictures of me for advertisements. At first it was innocent. He would have me look at and play with his hamster. Eventually, he worked, little by little to do things that no grown man should do to a little girl. I felt broken, vulnerable and worthless. Having been exposed to pornography before I could read, I knew that what was happening to me was wrong. One of the things I do remember is thinking, *Where are my parents? Why aren't they here protecting me, a 5-year-old, little girl?*

I felt broken, vulnerable and worthless.

Unfortunately, the door was now open for additional violators to come along and take advantage of me as well in many different situations over the years. It wasn't until I had been a Christian for 28 years that the Lord finally said to me, *"It's time to work on this area."* At first, I had no idea what He was talking about. I had already spoken upabout my abusers and forgiven them all. What I didn't realize was that nightmares I was having were because of the sexual abuse I had endured as a child.

The Lord led me to a book called *Healing the Wounded Heart: Removing Obstacles to Intimacy with God.* by Thom Gardner, which opened my eyes to my need for deliverance. If my mind was a house, I had given Jesus access to every room except one. That door was closed, boarded up, and marked off with skulls, crossbones and a sign that said, *"Do Not Enter!"*

As the Lord patiently walked me through deliverance, He showed me two different visions. In the first vision, I was deep in a dark cave and He was standing at the opening beckoning me to come out to Him. *"It's not safe in there."* He declared.

Initially, I refused. I said, *"I can't! Come in here and protect me."*

He responded, *"I can't protect you in there, you must come out here to me."*

Eventually, I did come out. It was just in the nick of time! As soon as I reached for His hand, he pulled me quickly to His bosom and held me tightly as the cave imploded behind me, but I was safe in His arms.

In the second vision, I was in a dinky, dingy boat that was in pieces. I was trying desperately to hold everything together with my hands and feet to keep it afloat, while next to me was Jesus, standing on the bow of an enormous yacht beckoning me to Him. This time, there was less hesitation.

After the visions, there was a final step. It was the night I nearly lost my mind! The nightmares were especially tormenting. They not only woke me up, but they didn't stop even after I was awake. They just kept coming. They would not stop. With every tormenting thought, I would give an audible rebuke as loud as I could without waking up my two young children. *"I rebuke that thought in the name of Jesus!"* After battling the bombardment of thoughts all night, they finally stopped, and, even though I was physically exhausted, I was free! The process was long, but thank God He restored my joy through freedom from the sexual abuse I experienced as a child.

Loss of Freedom

Bound to be Free

Therefore, if the Son makes you free, you shall be free
indeed.

(JOHN 8:36)

I remember Nov. 6, 2009, like it was yesterday. That day was my 38th birthday. I did not have big plans. I quit going out a few years before when I decided to give my life to Jesus. I had traded my days of drugs, alcohol, partying and promiscuity for Bible study, church choir and weekly church services. I was happier than ever being away from that "old way of life." I was no longer masking the pain from feeling unloved, rejected, abandoned and unwanted. I was free, or so I thought.

It was mid-day and I received a phone call from a close friend inviting me out for my birthday. I did not have anyone to watch my 9-year-old daughter, so I did not plan to go. Unfortunately, it seems when we are trying to live right; the wrong thing is always easy. My daughter's father, who was rarely available, offered to keep her that night so I could enjoy a night out for my birthday. Without giving it a second thought, I called up my friend and quickly accepted.

You see there was nothing wrong with going out to dinner and to hear some great music. Except for us, it was a bar and a club. What was I thinking? Or maybe I wasn't! The draw to the old way of life sucked me in like I had never left.

When we arrived at the nightclub, I was already having a great time from the drinks at the bar. My friend and I decided we would dance, and that is where I caught the club owner's eye. Whatever we wanted was ours at no cost. I do remember that, but I do not remember much else except being carried to the car by staff. Thankfully my friend had chosen to be the designated driver. Looking back, neither of us should have driven anything that night! Luckily, her house was just 15 minutes away. When we made it to her house, we laughed, talked and then she went to the restroom, then bed.

I made it to the exit of her neighborhood when I saw them, two flashing red lights.

It was at this point that I decided I was going to drive myself home. I grabbed my purse, threw my shoes in the car and headed for home. I made it to the exit of her neighborhood when I saw them, two flashing red lights. I was pulled over, failed a sobriety test and awoke in jail.

Upon arriving at the jail, I was booked and placed in a holding tank with prostitutes, drug addicts, intoxicated people—all people who were just like the "old me."

It was in this cell when I came face to face with the real me—the me that I was running from. I saw the hidden broken me that no one else could see. After 36 hours I was released on my own recognizance and at the mercy of the local court system.

I was reminded daily of the failure I was as a believer in Christ and as a mother. I didn't believe anyone could love me; I mean who could love a person like me? I let lies of the enemy do a number on me. My life consisted of months of deep depression, condemnation, secrecy, going to court, blowing into a breathalyzer to start my car and paying the court thousands of dollars.

How could the "good Christian" I thought I was find myself in a situation like this? I could not live with myself for failing my faith and my family. My prideful self did not want anyone to see that I was less than perfect, so I put up a façade. I did not like or love myself during this period of my life and figured out why no one else seemed to either. I was having a major Pity Party, and I was the guest of honor.

Thankfully, there was something inside of me that tugged, saying, *"make a choice which way will you go; you have to choose to be free or to be bound."* It was not easy, but after a few months I began to read the Word of God again. I searched the Bible for scriptures that were relevant to me. I began to say them out loud until I believed them. It was in God's Word that I was found. No longer did I have to put on a mask. I was free to be me! I will never forget that birthday, but not for the reason you may think. I believe that setback is what propelled me into a future of freedom. I had to be bound in order to be free!

LOSS OF A DREAM

Family or Fiancé

∽

The LORD is close to the brokenhearted; he rescues those
whose spirits are crushed.
(PSALM 34:18)

This was not the day I had imagined it would be. It was supposed to be a celebration. It was supposed to be glorious. Our family and friends were supposed to be there. I was supposed to have the day of my dreams. But it was not to be. Yes, I was married to the love of my life, and I was elated to be his wife, but I had lost my family in the process. Instead of a day of pure joy, I was heartbroken, and filled with uncertainty about our future. Not the best way to start a life together.

Ed and I were two days from graduating from college, but we had decided weeks earlier that we would be getting married in spite of my parents disapproval. It wasn't that we hadn't tried to honor my parents. We had dated for two years before my parents even acknowledged Ed as my boyfriend. When they finally invited him to our home for dinner, we announced our engagement, and Ed asked for my father's blessing over our impending marriage. My dad refused to give us his blessing, and he told us that without his approval,

our marriage would not be blessed. He spent the next hour or so explaining his position, but honestly, I can't remember what he said. The rest of that evening was a blur.

In spite of my parents' disapproval, Ed and I began to plan our wedding. Yes, we wanted my parents' approval and support, but it wasn't required. We were convinced that our Heavenly Father had given us His approval to move forward with our marriage. We didn't need to wait until my parents finally got on board. After several weeks of planning, my father realized that we were still determined to be married.

One day he called my dorm and told me that if Ed and I were married, the family would not be attending the wedding. I was devastated! What could I do? I sat in my dorm and cried. I was so confused. What was the right thing to do? I had tried so hard to be the good daughter that my parents wanted me to be. I had made the good grades. I performed well in sports. I was a leader in my sorority. I sought to be a good Christian. Still, I wasn't good enough. This wonderful, kind-hearted man that had captured my heart was still on the outside of my family. Instead of seeing him for the person he was, Ed was accused of being the cause of division within our family, and I was compared to a silly woman being carried away by her passions. They were wrong. I was simply a young woman who loved a man. We were young adults who were ready to commit ourselves to one another. That's not evil.

I had tried so hard to be the good daughter that my parents wanted me to be.

There came a moment when I had to choose between two things that no 21-year-old (or any person) should have to choose between—my fiancé and my family. It felt so unfair that I had to make this choice. Life was NOT supposed to be this way. No one should have to choose the love of their life over their family. But I did.

I chose to marry Ed two days before graduating from college. My decision led to my dad telling me to pack up my belongings and leave. It led to my family not celebrating my graduation from college with me. It led to my first Thanksgiving away from my family. And it led to a long road to restoration.

I began the process of restoration by reaching out to my family about a month after Ed and I were married in order to ask for their forgiveness. I knew they were very hurt and felt that I had betrayed them. I still loved my family and I wanted them in my life in spite of everything. I was sorry I had caused them so much pain. Little by little God healed our relationship. Eventually, my family was able to accept Ed as my husband and see the wonderful person he truly is.

Ed and I have our own family now. We have four children—

two boys and two girls. We have been graced by God to have a wonderful, loving family. In 2019, we are celebrating 25 years of marriage. Our God has taken the bitterness of our beginning and made it a sweet testimony of His redeeming power. No, my wedding day was not the day I had dreamed it would be, but my Heavenly Father has given me something far better. A beautiful life with a wonderful man.

Loss of Significance

Rainbow in the Sky

Now may the God of hope fill you with all joy and peace in believing, so that you will abound in hope by the power of the Holy Spirit.

(Romans 15:13)

I walked down the hallway of my house hoping that I wouldn't be faced with the sign posted on the door. As I slowly approached, there it was...the warning, "DO NOT DISTURB!" In smaller letters underneath, it read, "unless you are bleeding or dying." I turned around with my head hung heavy and my eyes fixed to the floor. There was hardly a day that I had come home from school and that note wasn't hanging on her door. I knew the drill. Just put the work that I did at school under the door and anything that needed to be signed and walk away.

What else could I do to get her attention? I had made all A's on my tests and had completed all my homework without any assistance. I had glowing reviews from all my teachers. I was obedient and did my chores and even learned how to cook for myself even if it was only ramen noodles. It was food.

Tears streamed across my face and another piece of my heart broke. I began to wonder if my existence even mattered. No one would even notice if I was gone. My dad lived states away and never called or visited. My younger half-brother moved to live with his dad in another state. I was alone.

I headed outside to the backyard and was comforted by my faithful swing. For some reason, I never felt alone when I was swinging. I would dream. Dreaming was my escape from reality. I could clearly see my husband and my two children, a girl first and then a boy. I was surrounded by their love. This dream kept me alive.

I ran inside and grabbed a razor from the bathroom and returned to my swing.

This day was different. My dreaming was surrounded by darkness. I couldn't shake the thoughts of my insignificance. I wanted to die. Death's warm embrace enveloped me and the sign on the door flashed in my mind "...unless *you are bleeding or dying*." A small whisper spoke, "You'll never be significant. Don't bother trying. Just give up."

I ran inside and grabbed a razor from the bathroom and returned to my swing. I put the razor to my wrist. As much as I wanted to rip my wrist to shreds, something inside me wouldn't allow it. There wasn't a voice this time, just a force that wouldn't let my hands apply pressure to my skin. I was reminded of the dream. I was reminded of my future. I was reminded that I had a purpose.

Childhood memories are an interesting part of an adult life that can give clues into the person they become. For years I was haunted by memories of my past, uncertain as to how they fit into the worldview I had developed and the ways in which I behaved. I was so curious about this that I decided to study the human mind and human behavior while in college and majored in Psychology and then went on to get a graduate degree in Counseling.

I continued to battle the lies that I wasn't significant and no matter how hard I tried I could never be enough. At the age of 20, my life was spiraling out of control. I was going through episodes of depression more frequently, and I couldn't keep up the level of performance required to be noticed. I slowly sank into the belief that I was worthless and this world would be better off without me. I didn't care anymore, and piece by piece I gave up. I lost my will to live.

My dream of having a husband and two children, a girl first and then a boy, came true, but the lie of my insignificance was rooted so deeply that I began believing that my family would be better off without me.

As I entered my 33rd year of life, I came to a crossroad. My dad had committed suicide on his birthday, and his son, my half-brother, died one month prior from a drug overdose. Even though I wasn't in a relationship with either one, I knew that this would be my fate unless there was some kind of divine intervention.

The following year The Divine intercepted my life. As I lay on a beach in the depths of my own personal hell, I reached to the Creator and asked Him to save me. I knew He heard me when a rainbow appeared in the sky over the ocean. Piece by piece His Peace restored me, delivered me, and He adopted me as His own. I am a daughter of the Most High King, and He calls me His beloved! He breathed His life into me, and I am the apple of His eye!

My life is significant, and its purpose is to bring hope and joy to the world around me.

Loss of Identity

Losing Big Two

I have been crucified with Christ, and it is no longer I who
live, but Christ lives in me, and the life which I now live in
the flesh I live by faith in the Son of God, who loved me and
gave Himself up for me.

(GALATIANS 2:20)

This is a story that my twin would love to tell. One morning we were having an argument about which one of us would go outside to see what all the commotion was about on June 19, 1952. She would say that I kicked her out; therefore, she became the first born with all the so-called power. Our first argument, which ended with me kicking her, would be the last time that I would ever strike her, but not the last time we would argue.

We were joyfully greeted by our big brother who was turning 2 in two days. He was excited to have two sisters! When neighbors asked him what our names were, he said, Big Two and Little Two because there are two of them! Being the last born, I received the nickname Little Two.

We had to dress alike every day for school. No arguments there. Whatever Big Two wanted to wear is what we wore. We shared a car together in high school—no arguments there. Wherever Big Two wanted to go, I would go along.

It was at about age 16 when the arguments started. Big Two loved to fudge on the truth a little bit, and I would try to hold her accountable. For instance, we would come home from the parade and she would say that we saw the largest balloon ever. I would say that it was not the largest balloon we had ever seen, and she would say it was the largest. I would remind her of the balloons we saw at the circus the year before and say they were larger. She would say they were not. And on and on until my mother would say that she had heard enough.

People always asked us how it felt to have a twin, and my answer was always the same. Much like having a sister—someone you can trust always. Another question was ***do you feel each other's pain?*** Always the answer was no, until Big Two was in a car accident. She had to be airlifted from the crash site and received over 100 stitches in her head. Unbelievably, I felt the pain in my head before I knew what was happening. My head was throbbing by the time I reached the hospital to be by her side.

Another time, Big Two was to be admitted to the hospital for an overnight stay to have her medicine regulated. I was going to the hospital just to hang out and keep her company. When she arrived at the hospital, she suffered a heart attack during admission and was put on life support. I had started to feel anxious before leaving work to go to the hospital and was shocked to learn she was in ICU. I was not able to see her for two hours after getting to the hospital. I prayed the entire time waiting for visitors' hours before seeing her.

When I got to her bed, I was in tears. She pulled the tube out of her mouth when she saw me crying and said to me what a nurse had told her earlier. "JC punched your timecard, but the angels in heaven weren't ready for you yet." The hospital records show that she died for seven minutes, and she said that she saw the brightest light ever at the end of a tunnel.

The stage 4 cancer diagnosis came in March of 2013. She spent 40 days in the hospital. I never left her side during her hospital stay. I would read Scripture and sing to her, and we would pray and worship each day at the hospital.

"JC punched your timecard, but the angels in heaven weren't ready for you yet."

The doctors and nurses would join in with us some days. Gospel music was always playing.

Toward the end, I wanted the nurse to remove the tubes from her throat because she did not want them and had taken them out herself on several occasions. She had screamed out in a very loud tone, "No!" Before that she had not spoken for several days and was just lying there with her eyes closed. I knew that it was too late, and she was too weak to conquer. Yet I held onto hope until the very end.

When the nurse told me that she could not remove the tubes because she was dying, I felt a lump in my throat that would not go away. I had slept the night before holding her hand to keep her from taking the tube out herself. When the chaplain came and prayed with us, I wanted to cry out to the Lord, but the lump in my throat prevented it. When she was pronounced dead, the lump was still there and prevented me from crying out also. I was not able to speak above a whisper for several days. Eating and sleeping also became difficult for me.

When I lost my twin, I lost my identity. I was no longer Little Two.

It took time, but eventually I regained my joy and identity as I stopped focusing on the loss. Instead, I began to focus on the beautiful life she lived. I started a scholarship fund in her honor for the graduating seniors from the public high school in our town. I began to speak about the wonderful memories I had with her, and God used that to restore my joy! I am grateful for the time God allowed us to be together as twins.

Loss of a Son

The Fight for My Life

Weeping may last for the night,
But a shout of joy comes in the morning.
(PSALM 30:5)

It was a typical summer day. My husband had taken our three younger children to their Vacation Bible School, and I was left home with my oldest son who was 13. I decided to relax a little in bed and write in my journal. We had been experiencing the normal struggles of a young family— finances and raising children. Soon I drifted off to sleep. An hour or so later, I felt something on my bottom behind me. I thought it was our little Maltese dog. Then I remembered that he was too short to jump onto the bed and we always had to pick him up. I was confused as to what it was, so I awoke completely alert to something I could not believe. My 13-year-old son was standing next to my bed completely naked and erect. It was him that I felt behind me!

I immediately jumped to my feet and said in a serious steady tone *"What are you doing?"*

No response as he stared blankly ahead, eyes fixated on something.

So I said again a little louder, my tone now more intense, *"What are you doing?"*

Still no response while my heart rate began to rapidly increase. We never made eye contact, but by then I was frantic and yelled in a panicked voice *"What are your doing?"*

He lay next to the door crying out in a strange voice, "Let me explain!"

He still did not respond, but I noticed it looked as if his eyes rolled into the back of his head.

The door to my room was right next to my bed. I pushed him and began using all my strength and the door to try to push him out of the room. Thirteen-year-old boys are strong. By then he was already taller than me and probably stronger. It was a battle hard fought by us both, but somehow, by the grace of God, I was finally able to get him out. I immediately closed the door and locked it. He did not move. He lay next to the door crying out in a strange voice, *"Let me explain!"*

I ran into my bathroom and called my husband on my cell phone, my heart still racing. I told him that something bad had happened and he needed to come home immediately. I would not tell him what it was. Later he told me that he broke every traffic law trying to make it home to me. He could tell it was serious by the sound of my voice.

Before my husband arrived, I heard the front door slam and knew that my son had left. I unlocked my door and peeked out to make sure there was no sign of him before going back into my bathroom and sitting on the floor—a crying, huddled heap of fear, anguish and despair. That is where my husband found me.

The District Attorney ended up pressing attempted sexual assault charges against my son when he admitted that he had been in the bathroom experimenting with himself, and came into my room to assault me. I remember making my victim's impact statement at the sentencing. The judge, my son, husband and attorneys were all present. I talked about bringing my son into our home at age 7 and how joyful, proud and thankful I was to be his mom, but how that had all changed the moment he attempted to violate me—his mother for the last six years. I was devastated!

Everything changed—I mean everything! Before this I was fearless! Need a 2 a.m. trip to Walmart for more snacks while we are watching movies? No problem. I was your girl! Now I lived in fear. I could no longer run out to the store at night to pick up a few items for meals the following day for fear that I would be accosted and raped. I remember taking a shower and thinking that my neighbor would break into my home and sexually assault me. I struggled with anxiety for months even years after that incident.

However the people that suffered most were my other two sons. Even though they were just little boys, I irrationally became fearful of them. When my husband would leave, I would often lock myself in my room for hours, especially at night. I did not want them to walk behind me because that is how my son had approached me—from behind.

Through therapy we learned that he had been sexually abused by a male, his caretaker in his foster home, prior to coming to live with us. We did not know this before, and he showed no signs of this behavior until he hit puberty.

We had visitation with my older son, and I was extremely fearful of him. When he was released after serving time in a juvenile detention center, I was still fearful of him and refused to be left alone with him. If my husband left, my son had to go with him—no exceptions.

However, through some miracle and a whole lot of prayer, God began to heal me. It took a long time, but now almost eight years later, my son and I have a wonderful relationship. God restored everything about it! I can hug him and allow him to hug me just as a mother and son should show affection to each other without the fear of what happened in the past. I lost my son for a season, but I am thankful that God's restoration power and joy is real and I have him back now!

LOSS OF TRUST

Broken Vows

How blessed is the man who has made the Lord his trust,
and has not turned to the proud, nor to those who lapse into
falsehood.

(PSALM 40:4)

The year 2017 was a year of extreme loneliness, trauma and desperation as I tried to fix my marriage in any way that I knew how. My husband travelled one to three weeks at a time coming home for less than a week before suddenly leaving again with no notice. I could not figure out why he had no desire to connect with me after being gone for weeks at a time. I tried heart-to-heart talks, I tried having him listen to CDs and read books. He went to church week after week. I tried being a better wife. I tried fighting, begging and giving him whatever he wanted. I needed him to love me. It was a time when I was stuck in a compulsive need to fix him so that I could feel better. I was not able to take good care of myself. But somehow all of this suffering and extreme pain was just what was needed.

One day I noticed that my husband's phone was off. He said he was doing this so that he would focus on his family on Sundays. Well the next Sunday when I mentioned that he didn't turn it off he denied saying he did that on Sundays. This was suspicious to me. The next morning I asked to look through his phone. He agreed to let me, but he had to stand over me the entire time. The longer he stood over me and the more defensive he became saying things like, "I am tired of being treated like a child!" Soon my husband was trying to grab the phone from my hands. At that moment I knew. I knew he was cheating on me.

I was shaking uncontrollably off and on for days.

I spent the next week trying to convince him in anyway I could that he could tell me the truth and that it would save our marriage. Finally, on Christmas Eve he let me know he had been unfaithful to me many times in our marriage and even had a longer relationship with a woman the past three months. I was devastated to say the least and in so much trauma.

The post-traumatic stress disorder I experienced was horrendous. I was shaking uncontrollably for days. Months later we did a therapeutic disclosure with polygraph where I learned that he was unfaithful on and off throughout our entire 18 years of marriage with 2017 being the first time he had full blown relationships with other women.

I was in so much pain. The pain was unbearable. I always believed in God, but where was He now? I no longer had any control over my life.

Did my husband ever love me? How could anyone love me? What hope did I have left? This pain led me to get help. I had kids to be there for. I couldn't stay like this forever. I couldn't talk to my family or friends. They would just give me advice and that is not what I needed. After consulting my pastors, I was referred to a counselor. So we did what was available and where God led us. My husband and I both entered into recovery programs. My husband entered recovery for sex addiction, while I entered recovery for being a survivor of infidelity. I found myself in a recovery whirlwind. I was meeting new friends in recovery groups and in therapy groups along with trying new therapists and life coaching. I was attending intensive therapy and retreats out of town. I was in a world I didn't even know existed. I even found people from my own church in this world of infidelity recovery.

But it was in this new world of recovery where I found authenticity, true love of myself, hope, and best of all, God. I thought because I was a church-goer and I prayed and because I raised my family in the faith, that I was all set. But little did I know that I was missing a very important piece of the puzzle. That piece was self-worth. I had learned to "love your neighbor as yourself," but what I didn't learn all those years was that loving myself meant understanding my worth in the eyes of God and that I matter. I learned that until I could learn this, I could not love anyone more than I love myself. And while I had been a church-goer, by missing this important part, I was only changing my behaviors and not my heart. No matter how much I tried to love, it would be limited until I had a very real relationship with God as my real Daddy.

As for me and my husband, although I lost trust in him, I have gained trust in the love I have for myself and from God. Learning who I am and how loved I am allows me to love my husband more than I ever have and no longer be completely shattered by his poor choices in the future. I know now that I will be okay no matter what happens to my marriage. I have never felt so free in my life, and everyday I keep walking the recovery journey with God the freer I am to love God, love my neighbor, and myself. Yes I have to learn how to fall in love all over again, but this time to the REAL prince—Jesus who already fought and died for me and to my real father- God the Father, and the Holy Spirit would walk hand in hand with me.

PART IV:
IT'S YOUR TURN

It is your turn to unmask yourself! Use the following pages to write down your story of loss. Remember, we have ALL suffered losses. I would love to hear your story if you would like to share. Please email me at davis.tamatha@gmail.com. There may just be a Joyous Journey of Loss, Part II!

____

____

____

____

____

____

____

____

PART V:
THE TOOLBOX

Toolbox A
Praising Scriptures

Sing to the Lord, *all the earth;*
Proclaim good tidings of His salvation from day to day. Tell of
    His glory among the nations,
His wonderful deeds among all the peoples. Ascribe to the Lord,
    O families of the peoples,
Ascribe to the Lord *glory and strength.*
Ascribe to the Lord *the glory due His name;*
Bring an offering, and come before Him;
Worship the Lord *in holy array.*
Tremble before Him, all the earth.

—1 Chronicles 16:23, 24, 28, 29

Exalt the Lord *our God*
And worship at His footstool;
Holy is He.

—Psalm 99:5

*Ascribe to the L*ORD *the glory due to His name;*
*Worship the L*ORD *in holy array.*

—PSALM 29:2

Therefore, since we receive a kingdom which cannot be shaken,
let us show gratitude, by which we may offer to God an accept-
able service with reverence and awe.

—HEBREWS 12:28, 29

*Shout joyfully to the L*ORD*, all the earth.*
*²Serve the L*ORD *with gladness;*
Come before Him with joyful singing.
*³Know that the L*ORD *Himself is God;*
It is He who has made us, and not we ourselves;
We are His people and the sheep of His pasture.
⁴Enter His gates with thanksgiving
And His courts with praise.
Give thanks to Him, bless His name.
*⁵For the L*ORD *is good;*
His lovingkindness is everlasting
And His faithfulness to all generations.

—PSALM 100

And he said with a loud voice, "Fear God, and give Him glory,
because the hour of His judgment has come; worship Him
who made the heaven and the earth and sea and springs of
waters.

—REVELATION 14:7

Let the name of God be blessed forever and ever, For wisdom and power belong to Him.

—DANIEL 2:20

I shall make mention of the loving kindnesses of the LORD, the praises of the LORD,

—ISAIAH 63:7A

We give thanks to You, O God, we give thanks,
For Your name is near;
Men declare Your wondrous works.

—PSALM 75:1

Toolbox B

How to Pray the Names of God

Jehovah-Nissi, You are my Victory, my Banner, and my Standard. Your banner over me is love. When the enemy comes on like a flood, You lift up a standard against him. Hallowed be Thy name!

Jehovah-Shalom, I bless your name. You are my Peace—the peace which transcends all understanding, which garrisons and mounts guard over my heart and mind in Christ Jesus. Hallowed be Thy name!

I bless you Jehovah-Tsidkenu, my Righteousness. Thank you for becoming sin for me that I might become the righteousness of God in Christ Jesus. Hallowed be Thy name!

Hallelujah to Jehovah-Shammah, the One who will never leave or forsake me. You are always there. Hallowed be Thy name!

I worship and adore you El-Elyon, the Most High God, Who is the first cause of everything, the everlasting God, the great God, the living God, the merciful God, the faithful God, the mighty

God. You are Truth, Justice, Righteousness, and Perfection. Hallowed be Thy name!

Father, You have exalted above all else Your name and Your Word. Your Word was made flesh and dwelt among us, and His name is Jesus! Hallowed be Thy name!

In Jesus' sweet, beautiful, matchless name I pray, Amen.[2]

---

[2]Adapted from *Prayers That Avail Much*, Germaine Copeland, Handover, MD: Harrison House Publishers, 2005.

Toolbox C

Put On the Armor of God

In the name of Jesus, I put on the whole armor of God, that I may be able to stand against the wiles of the devil; for I wrestle not against flesh and blood, but against principalities, powers, the rulers of the darkness of this world, and spiritual wickedness in high places.

Therefore, I take unto myself the whole armor of God, that I may be able to withstand in the evil day, and having done all, to stand. I stand therefore, having my loins girt about with truth. Your Word, Lord, which is truth, contains all the weapons of my warfare, which are not carnal, but mighty in God to the pulling down of strongholds.

I have on the breastplate of righteousness, which is faith and love. My feet are shod with the preparation of the Gospel of peace. In Christ, I have peace and pursue peace with all men.

I am a minister of reconciliation, proclaiming the good news of the Gospel.

I have on the belt of truth. I do not listen to the lies of the enemy. I know that when he speaks he is speaking his native language, so I fill my mind with the truth of your word.

I take the shield of faith, wherewith I am able to quench the fiery darts of the wicked, the helmet of salvation, the Sword of the Spirit, which is the Word of God. In the face of trials, tests, temptations and tribulation, I cut to pieces the snare of the enemy by speaking the Word of God! Greater is He that is in me than he that is in the world!

I will pray at all times—on every occasion, in every season—in the Spirit, with all manner of prayer and entreaty. To that end I will keep alert and watch with strong purpose and perseverance! Thank you, Lord for the armor. In Jesus name, Amen.

Toolbox D

Confessing God's Word Over Your Life

I declare that this is the day that God made and I will rejoice and be glad in it.

—Psalm 118:24

I am fearfully and wonderfully made.

—Psalm 139:14

I am blessed going in and coming out.

—Deuteronomy 28:6

No weapon formed against me will be able to prosper.

—Isaiah 54:17

God works all things together for my good.

—ROMANS 8:28

All my family will be taught of the Lord and great will be their peace.

—ISAIAH 54:13

I am the head and not the tail, above only and not beneath.

—DEUTERONOMY 28:13

God surrounds me with His favor.

—PSALM 54:12

Toolbox E

Battlefield Scriptures

Put on the full armor of God, so that you will be able to stand firm against the schemes of the devil. [12] *For our struggle is not against flesh and blood, but against the rulers, against the powers, against the world forces of this darkness, against the spiritual forces of wickedness in the heavenly places.* [13] *Therefore, take up the full armor of God, so that you will be able to resist in the evil day, and having done everything, to stand firm.* [14] *Stand firm therefore, having girded your loins with truth, and having put on the breastplate of righteousness,* [15] *and having shod your feet with the preparation of the gospel of peace;* [16] *in addition to all, taking up the shield of faith with which you will be able to extinguish all the flaming arrows of the evil one.* [17] *And take the helmet of salvation, and the sword of the Spirit, which is the word of God.*

—EPHESIANS 6:11-17

But in all these things we overwhelmingly conquer through Him who loved us.

—ROMANS 8:37

Fight the good fight of faith; take hold of the eternal life to which you were called, and you made the good confession in the presence of many witnesses.

—TIMOTHY 6:12

The Lord shall cause your enemies who rise up against you to be defeated before you; they will come out against you one way and will flee before you seven ways.

—DEUTERONOMY 28:7

For You have girded me with strength for battle; You have subdued under me those who rose up against me.

—PSALM 18:39

Through You we will push back our adversaries; Through Your name we will trample down those who rise up against us.

—PSALM 44:5

Have I not commanded you? Be strong and courageous! Do not tremble or be dismayed, for the Lord your God is with you wherever you go.

—JOSHUA 1:9

For the weapons of our warfare are not of the flesh, but divinely powerful for the destruction of fortresses.

—2 CORINTHIANS 10:4

Blessed be the Lord, my rock, Who trains my hands for war, And my fingers for battle.

—PSALM 144:1

Be of sober spirit, be on the alert. Your adversary, the devil, prowls around like a roaring lion, seeking someone to devour.

—1 PETER 5:8,9

But in all these things we overwhelmingly conquer through Him who loved us.

—ROMANS 8:37

The thief comes only to steal and kill and destroy; I came that they may have life, and have it abundantly.

—JOHN 10:10

Submit therefore to God. Resist the devil and he will flee from you.

—JAMES 4:7

Behold, I have given you authority to tread on serpents and scorpions, and over all the power of the enemy, and nothing will injure you.

—LUKE 10:19

"No weapon that is formed against you will prosper; And every tongue that accuses you in judgment you will condemn. This is the heritage of the servants of the Lord, And their vindication is from Me," declares the Lord.

—ISAIAH 54:17

But thanks be to God, who gives us the victory through our Lord Jesus Christ.

—1 CORINTHIANS 15:57

www.ingramcontent.com/pod-product-compliance
Lightning Source LLC
Chambersburg PA
CBHW032255070726
47590CB00016B/2805